CONTENTS

The Author

David L. Silvernail is Assistant Professor of Curriculum and Instruction in the College of Education at the University of Southern Maine, Gorham.

The Consultants

The following educators have reviewed the manuscript and provided helpful comments and suggestions:

Patricia C. Deletetsky, Second Grade Teacher, Fairfield School, Saco, Maine

Marc W. Galbraith, Social Studies Teacher, Scarborough High School, Scarborough, Maine

Alan D. Rozinsky, Psychology Instructor, Weaver High School, Hartford, Connecticut

Robert Strandquist, English Teacher, Roseau High School, Roseau, Minnesota.

What Research Says to the Teacher

Teaching Styles as Related to Student Achievement

by David L. Silvernail

National Education Association
Washington, D.C.

Stock No. 1049-3-00

Note

The opinions expressed in this publication should not be construed as representing the policy or position of the National Education Association. Materials published as part of the What Research Says to the Teacher series are intended to be discussion documents for teachers who are concerned with specialized interests of the profession. (779, 883)

Acknowledgments

The following materials are reprinted with permission from the sources indicated: Flanders Interaction Analysis Categories (FIAC) from p. 14 of *The Role of the Teacher in the Classroom* by Amidon and Flanders. Copyright © 1963 by P. S. Amidon and Associates, Association for Productive Teaching, 1966 Benson Ave., St. Paul, Minn. 55116. Excerpts from Jere E. Brophy and Carolyn M. Evertson, *Learning from Teaching: A Developmental Perspective* (pp. 94, 91, 91-92, 82, and 106). Copyright © 1976 by Allyn and Bacon, Inc., Boston. Excerpts from N. Bennett, *Teaching Styles and Pupil Progress* (pp. 45, 47, and 101). Copyright © 1976 by Harvard University Press, Cambridge, Mass.

Library of Congress Cataloging in Publication Data

Silvernail, David L.
    Teaching styles as related to student achievement.

    "What research says to the teacher, special report."
    Bibliography: p.
    1. Teaching. 2. Academic achievement. 3. Teacher-student relationships.
4. Interaction analysis in education. I. What research says to the teacher.
II. Title.
LB1025.2.S52   371.1'02   79-12804
ISBN 0-8106-1049-3

 4

INTRODUCTION

In recent years our schools have received renewed criticism by educators and noneducators alike. Many have become alarmed by reports of declining achievement levels in our youth. Studies have revealed a fairly consistent fifteen-year decline in many standard achievement test scores and an increase in national illiteracy rates. These reports, coupled with community tax revolts and the enactment of public spending limitations, suggest that schools are moving into a period of closer scrutiny and reformation.

Many explanations have been offered for the drop in achievement test scores. Harnischfeger and Wiley (68)* suggest curricular changes, increased television viewing, and changing family configurations as possible explanations for the drop in scores. A blue ribbon panel chaired by former Secretary of Labor Willard Wirtz has identified several possible contributing factors such as compositional changes in tested groups, changing courses of study, declining educational standards, television, and the diminution in achievement motivation on the part of young people (183). A recent public opinion poll indicates that, for many, the causes are the lack of discipline, a de-emphasis on the basics, poor teaching, and a general decline in scholastic standards in our schools (57).

Whatever factor or combination of factors ultimately accounts for the decline, it is abundantly clear that many believe our schools are not doing an adequate job. Thus, it appears especially timely for us, as professional educators, to reexamine the effects of our teaching efforts.

What teaching activities enhance pupil learning? Are certain teaching styles and strategies more effective than others in helping youth increase their academic achievement? Many textbook answers are offered to these questions, but to use an old adage, the proof of the pudding is in the eating. How well do these textbook theories hold up in the real world of the classroom? Are they supported by empirical research? The purpose of this publication is to report and summarize the research findings with respect to these questions. What follows is not a definitive answer, for the inherent complexity of the teaching act and the limitations of educational research preclude one. What the reader will find is a discussion of the evidence that suggests the type of relationships which exist between certain teaching styles and academic achievement.

In reviewing the research, the author has relied and expanded upon the work of previous writers. The topic of teaching effectiveness has produced a voluminous amount of research of varying quality and

*Numbers in parentheses appearing in the text refer to the Selected References beginning on page 31.

importance in recent years. Reviews of this research by Rosenshine and Furst (141) and by Dunkin and Biddle (44) have aided the author in identifying key studies. The more recent findings discussed in the following pages build upon these earlier works to expand our understanding of the relationships of teaching styles to pupil learning.

HISTORICAL PERSPECTIVE

The systematic study of teaching effectiveness has a rather sporadic history. Medley (109) reports that the first study appeared in 1896 (96). Beginning with this study and continuing into the mid-1950s, several researchers focused on student perceptions of "good" teachers. Good characteristics included such variables as teaching skills, knowledge of subject matter, enthusiasm, considerateness, and fairness in grading (71,96). These studies had one serious flaw, however. Medley (109) reports that none of them included any attempt to measure the effects of such teacher characteristics on pupil achievement.

In the 1930s, paralleling the beginnings of the child development movement, researchers began to take a more objective look at teaching effectiveness. After many false starts, direct observation instruments were developed and used to characterize teacher behavior (10,15,89,166). Generally, the early instruments were checklists or rating scales designed to identify globally defined traits. Although viewed by many as an improvement over earlier attempts to identify effective behaviors, the unreliability of the instruments and the general lack of interest in the research topic further delayed the development of objective, valid, and reliable methods of examining the effects of teaching styles and behaviors on pupil learning.

A renewed interest in the analysis of the teaching process came about in the 1960s. Soar (155) identifies 1958 and 1960 as key dates signaling the change. In 1958 Medley and Mitzel (110) published the Observation Schedule and Record (OScAR), and in 1960 Flanders (51) published the initial findings of his Interaction Analysis Categories system (FIAC). Both studies were based upon earlier attempts by Anderson (7) to study the effects of "dominative" versus "integrative" teacher behavior, and by Withall (184) to study the effects of "teacher-centered" and "learner-centered" classroom climates. The significance of these studies and of those by Medley and Mitzel, and Flanders was that each defined teacher behavior traits as composites of a number of specific behaviors that could be categorized, observed, and recorded. These studies led to the development of new observation instruments and new research methodologies which have resulted in many significant examinations of the effects of teaching styles on pupil achievement.

OVERVIEW

Given this brief historical perspective, let us now turn our attention to a discussion of the current state of the art. Has research identified the most effective teaching styles? In part, the answer lies in an understanding of the research methodologies used to study teacher effectiveness.

Basically, teaching effectiveness research focuses on one or more components of some model of the classroom teaching process. The most widely used model is one developed by Mitzel (118). Although refined and expanded upon by Dunkin and Biddle (44) and others, the basic model consists of four classes of variables: presage, context, process, and product. Presage and context variables include such things as the personality, knowledge, abilities, and status characteristics of teachers and pupils. Process variables describe the interactions of teacher and pupil behaviors, and product variables are primarily concerned with measures of pupil changes. Research designed to examine the relationships between teaching styles, strategies, and pupil learning involves both process and product variables.

Process-product studies usually involve two major steps: (1) the description of selected teaching/instructional activities; and (2) the correlation of this description with some measure of pupil outcome, that is, learning and/or attitudes. Before attempting to interpret the findings of these studies, we must take a closer look at each step.

The description step entails the use of a high-inference or low-inference-type instrument to characterize teacher-pupil classroom interactions (137,172). A low-inference instrument, such as an observation schedule, permits observers to categorize and count the frequency of certain events as they occur in the classroom. Hundreds of observation instruments have been developed, but the most widely used is the Flanders Interaction Analysis Categories system (FIAC) (51) referred to earlier. The ten categories and Flanders's description of each are given in Figure 1.

A questionnaire survey is an example of a high-inference instrument. Respondents are asked to describe their behavior or that of others. A majority of these instruments consist of a number of statements characterizing teacher and pupil behaviors and classroom interactions about which students are asked to indicate their perceptions. Many such instruments exist (66,161,162,176), but a representative example is the Classroom Environment Scale (CES) developed by Trickett and Moos (171). The ninety-item scale measures nine dimensions of classroom climate, including student involvement and affiliation, teacher support, task orientation, competition, classroom order and organization, rule clarity, teacher control and innovation.

FIGURE 1
Flanders Interaction Analysis Categories

Teacher Talk

1. *Accepts feeling.* Accepts and clarifies an attitude or a feeling tone of a pupil in a nonthreatening manner. Feelings may be positive or negative.

2. *Praises or encourages.* Praises or encourages pupil action or behavior. Jokes that release tension, but not at the expense of another individual; nodding head, or saying "Um hm?" or "Go on" are included.

3. *Accepts or uses ideas of pupils.* Clarifying, building, or developing ideas suggested by a pupil. Teacher extensions of pupil ideas are included, but as the teacher brings more of his own ideas into play, shift to category five.

4. *Asks questions.* Asking a question about content or procedure, based on teacher ideas, with the intent that a pupil will answer.

5. *Lecturing.* Giving facts or opinions about content or procedures; expressing *his own* ideas, giving *his own* explanation, or citing an authority other than a pupil.

6. *Giving directions.* Directions, commands, or orders to which a pupil is expected to comply.

7. *Criticizing or justifying authority.* Statements intended to change pupil behavior from nonacceptable to acceptable pattern; bawling someone out, stating why the teacher is doing what he is doing; extreme self-reference.

Pupil Talk

8. *Pupil-talk-response.* Talk by pupils in response to teacher. Teacher initiates the contact or solicits pupil statement or structures the situation. Freedom to express own ideas is limited.

9. *Pupil-talk-initiation.* Talk by pupils which they initiate. Expressing own ideas, initiating a new topic; freedom to develop opinions and a line of thought, like asking thoughtful questions; going beyond the existing structure.

Silence

10. *Silence or confusion.* Pauses, short periods of silence and periods of confusion in which communication cannot be understood by the observer. (51)

The second phase in process-product research involves correlating the data collected through the use of high- and low-inference instruments with some measure of pupil learning or attitude change. The purpose is to determine the degree of relationship between certain teacher behaviors/ teaching styles and student academic learning and/or attitude. A key fact to keep in mind is that phase two involves *correlating* process and product variables. Some experimental studies have been conducted, but an overwhelming majority of research in the area of teacher effectiveness is correlational in nature. The difference, and more importantly, the significance of this fact is that experimental studies are designed to establish *cause and effect;* that is, a specific teaching style *causes* certain pupil outcomes. Correlational studies, on the other hand, reveal only the presence or absence of a mutual relationship; that is, the presence of a specific teaching style is concomitant with certain pupil outcomes. Cause-and-effect relationships cannot be inferred from correlational findings. Thus, for instance, if teacher praise *correlates* with greater pupil learning, we cannot conclude that praise *causes* greater learning. This limitation does not destroy the value of correlational research. It merely mandates the use of caution in interpreting the results. Correlational findings do reveal which teaching styles are accompanied by pupil learning and consequently suggest strategies teachers can use to improve their effectiveness.

A final note of clarification is necessary before we turn our attention to the research findings. Process-product research has focused on both cognitive and affective outcomes. This publication will describe only those findings that deal with learning outcomes. Depending upon community and pupil needs and interests, and professional judgments, the affective outcomes of the school process may be equally or more important. But because of the increased public concern for academic achievement and the limited nature of this publication, only the research findings for teaching styles/strategies and pupil academic learning will be considered here.

Table 1 is designed as a thumbnail sketch of these findings which will be reviewed and summarized in the subsequent pages. The column on the left lists teaching variables; the columns on the right indicate the relationships of these variables to academic achievement. A plus sign (+) in both columns to the right indicates conflicting evidence.

TABLE 1

Relationships Between Teaching Variables and Pupil Achievement

Teaching Variable	Positive Relationship	Negative or No Relationship
1. *Globally Defined Teaching Styles*		
a. direct styles	+	+
b. indirect styles	+	+
c. flexible direct and indirect styles (curvilinear relationships)	+	
d. formal and mixed styles	+	
2. *Feedback*		
a. elaborate praise or criticism		+
b. simple praise	+	
c. teacher-initiated praise	+	
d. mild criticism/simple praise tied to SES and ability levels of students	+	
e. use of pupil ideas	+	
3. *Questioning Activities*		
a. frequency of questions	+	
b. different questioning patterns		+
c. seeking improved responses	+	+
d. type of questions (mixing cognitive level of questions)	+	
4. *Structuring Activities*		
a. lesson introductions	+	
b. reviewing	+	
c. providing content-relevant information	+	
d. pretests	+	+
e. behavior objectives	+	+
f. advance organizers	+	+

TABLE 1—*continued*

Teaching Variable	Positive Relationship	Negative or No Relationship
5. *Clarity*		
a. clarity of aims/presentation	+	
b. clear questions	+	
c. lesson/class organization	+	
6. *Task-Oriented Teaching Style*		
a. time on cognitive tasks	+	
b. businesslike teacher behavior	+	
7. *Enthusiasm*		
a. stimulating behavior	+	
b. use of gestures	+	
c. speech inflection variations	+	
8. *Reward Structures*		
a. individual competition	+	
b. cooperation structures	+	+
9. *Perceived Classroom Climate*		
a. involvement, affiliation, cohesiveness	+	
b. satisfying, difficult, rich environment	+	
c. apathy, friction, cliquishness, favoritism		+

GLOBALLY DEFINED TEACHING STYLES

Teaching styles may be characterized in a variety of ways. One way is according to instructional modes such as recitation and lecture, discussion, inquiry, or role-playing (86). Another is in terms of teaching models. Joyce and Weil (92) offer four broad categories of teaching models: social interaction, information processing, personal source, and behavior modification. Each category represents a relatively unique teaching style.

A popular way of characterizing teaching styles is in some dichotomous fashion. For instance, we read of authoritarian versus democratic styles (102), pupil-centered versus teacher-centered styles (184), and traditional versus progressive styles (117, 182). In terms of research, two dichotomies that have received a considerable amount of attention are (1) the direct and indirect teaching styles and (2) variations of the traditional and progressive styles.

Direct and Indirect Teaching Styles

Much of the research on the direct/indirect dichotomy is based on Flanders's work. Flanders postulates that pupil learning is affected by teacher influence in the classroom and that this influence is established through the teacher's verbal behavior. The two major types of influence are as follows:

> *Direct Influence* [which] consists of stating the teacher's own opinions or ideas, directing the pupil's action, criticizing his behavior, or justifying the teacher's authority or use of that authority.
>
> *Indirect Influence* [which] consists of soliciting the opinions or ideas of the pupils, applying or enlarging on those opinions or ideas, praising or encouraging the participation of pupils, or clarifying and accepting their feelings. (49)

Using these descriptions of direct and indirect influences and the Flanders Interaction Analysis schedule (FIAC) presented in Figure 1, many investigators have attempted to study the relationship between these broadly defined teaching styles and pupil learning (48, 54, 134, 151, 154). First, using Flanders's categories 1–4 to represent indirect influences and 5–7 to represent direct influences, researchers observe teachers in their classrooms and develop numerical profiles depicting different teaching styles. As an example, by counting the frequency of events in each category for a given time period (e.g., three class periods), a researcher can determine an indirect/direct numerical ratio—a number which represents the teacher's style. A number greater than one represents an indirect style and a number less than one represents a direct style. Using different I/D ratios developed in this fashion, researchers can then analyze the relationships between different teacher profiles (teaching styles) and pupil learning.

Which of the broadly defined teaching styles is related to greater academic achievement? The variety of methodologies and the fine distinctions between I/D ratios made by different researchers prevent a definitive answer. We do know that teachers tend to exhibit more direct rather than indirect influence in the classroom (48, 54, 133, 168). Flanders's work led him to postulate his so-called "law of two-thirds" (49). Dunkin and Biddle (44) describe this law as "two-thirds of the time spent in classrooms is devoted to talk, two-thirds of this talking time is occupied by the teacher, and two-thirds of teacher talk consists of direct influence." This pattern of influence is not a new phenomenon. No less than four researchers have found similar results in studies dating back as far as 1912 (19, 38, 79, 163). Additionally, we know that teachers exhibit greater indirectness with pupils of higher social classes and greater intelligence (76, 78). Male and female teachers appear to exercise the same type of influence (158). Not surprisingly, greater teacher indirectness is associated with greater pupil talk (4, 54, 159), and, in at least one study, greater teacher indirectness leads to more thought-provoking questions on the part of students (90).

With respect to academic learning, some research findings tend to support the superiority of the indirect style (48, 54, 84, 179). Samph (145) found that language development and overall achievement of sixth graders was greater for pupils exposed to an indirect teaching style. Similar results have been reported for junior high school students in mathematics, social studies, and language arts (48, 131). Indirectness also enhanced the achievement of secondary general science and chemistry students (29, 186), and Wolfson (186) concluded that secondary students retained more information when taught by indirect teachers.

Not all the evidence supports the effectiveness of the indirect teaching style, however. Several researchers report that "indirectness" is unrelated to pupil achievement, especially in the lower grades (1, 154, 157, 167). In studying secondary science, mathematics, and economics, Cook (37), Torrance (169), and Furst (54) respectively came to similar conclusions. Flanders (49), while finding general support for indirective styles, also reported mixed results in some cases. Powell (134), exploring the long-term effects of direct and indirect styles, discovered that the superior effects of exposure to indirect styles dissipated over time. Pupils learning from indirect-style teachers for the first three years of their schooling scored higher on arithmetic achievement tests, and about the same on reading achievements tests, as those learning from more directive teachers. But by the end of the fourth grade, there were no

13

significant differences* in the achievement of the two groups, regardless of the pupil's exposure to either direct or indirect teaching styles. Thus, indirectness does not appear to be superior in all cases.

Why the seemingly conflicting results? Rosenshine (140) suggests that it is inappropriate to compare those studies because of different methodologies and definitions used to identify the two globally defined styles. In some studies, only a fine line separated directive and indirective teachers; therefore, in reality researchers were assessing degrees of a particular style and not a dichotomous situation. The achievement potential of students may also offer a partial explanation. Tisher (168), studying ninth grade science studies, discovered that low achievers gained more when teachers exhibited greater indirectness behavior. Flanders explained his mixed results in terms of teacher flexibility, saying that although, in general, pupils in indirect classroom climates gained more than those in more direct climates, ". . . teachers who were able to provide flexible patterns of influence by shifting from indirect to direct with the passage of time created situations in which students learned more" (49).

Possibly, the explanation which has the most far-reaching implications comes from the work of Soar (152, 154). He attempted to assess the effectiveness of direct/indirect teaching styles on the achievement of fifty-five classrooms of third through sixth grade students. An analysis of the data on three measures of pupil growth (reading comprehension, vocabulary, and creativity) resulted in no clear evidence in favor of either direct or indirect styles. Attempting to resolve what appeared to be discrepancies in his findings, Soar hypothesized the existence of a curvilinear relationship between teacher indirectness and academic learning (155). Specifically, he hypothesized that the level of thinking/reasoning required in different learning tasks is related to different optimum levels of indirectness. Additionally, there is an upper limit to the degree of indirectness that is associated with pupil gains, and beyond that point pupils will actually learn less rather than more. Reanalysis of the original data confirmed the hypothesis. Growth in creativity, which required the most complex and abstract thinking on the part of the pupils, was basically linear and no optimum level of directness/indirectness was found. On the other hand, optimum levels were found for *less* complex and abstract thinking tasks (vocabulary) and for *least* abstract tasks (reading comprehension). On the basis of this study and others, Soar

---

*The word "significant" has a specific meaning in research. It refers to a judgment as to whether apparent differences are true or whether they merely result from chance. A finding of "no significant differences" means that apparent differences can be attributed to chance, and a finding of "significant differences" means that apparent differences are true differences; that is, too large to be reasonably attributed to chance.

14

postulated the generalization that a single teaching style is not appropriate for all learning tasks, and that the optimum level for each style differs depending upon the nature of the learning task.

Formal and Informal Teaching Styles

Researchers have also developed various traditional versus progressive dichotomies to study teaching effectiveness in the past fifteen years. The most recent, thorough, and systematic study is Bennett's work with the formal and informal dimension (20). Using definitions of ''traditional'' and ''progressive,'' Bennett broke the concepts down into their composite elements which then formed the content of a questionnaire given to a large representative sample of teachers. Cluster analysis of the data resulted in the creation of a typology of twelve teaching styles which depicted various points on the formal and informal continuum. Bennett describes the two styles at the ends of the continuum as follows:

Informal Style: These teachers favour integration of subject matter, and, unlike most other groups, allow pupil choice of work, whether undertaken individually or in groups. Most allow pupils choice of seating. Less than half curb movement and talk. Assessment in all its forms—tests, grading, and homework—appears to be discouraged. Intrinsic motivation is favoured. (20, p. 45)

Formal Style: None [teachers] favour an integrated approach. Subjects are taught separately by class teaching and individual work. None allow pupils choice of seating, and every teacher curbs movement and talk. These teachers are above average on all assessment procedures, and extrinsic motivation predominates. (20, p. 47)

Selecting a sample of third- and fourth-year primary teachers which reflected each of the twelve styles, Bennett followed the progress of their students for one year. Analysis of pre- and post-test achievement scores showed the following results:

Reading
1. Pupils taught by formal and mixed styles show significantly superior progress as compared with those taught by informal styles.
2. The effect is more noticeable in average and above-average achievers. Low-achieving boys in formal classrooms progress less well than expected, but this is not true of low-achieving formal girls. Above-average boys in informal classrooms markedly underachieve in comparison to boys of the same ability in mixed and formal classrooms.

Mathematics
1. Pupils taught by formal styles show significantly superior progress to that of those taught by mixed and informal styles.
2. The superiority exists at every level of achievement among boys

15

and girls, with the exception of the least able boys, who again progress less well than expected.

English
1. Pupils taught by formal styles show significantly superior progress as compared with those taught by mixed and informal styles. Mixed pupils also show progress significantly superior to that of informal pupils.
2. Formal boys gain higher scores at every level of achievement, with the exception of the least able. Mixed girls progress most below an English quotient of 100, beyond which formal girls show greatest progress. (20, p. 101)

Bennett's results thus reveal that pupils taught by formal styles, and in some cases mixed styles, made greater progress than those taught by informal styles. With a few exceptions, noticeably in reading, gains were consistent across pupil achievement levels.

Do these results conflict with the findings for direct and indirect teaching styles? Not necessarily. True, in terms of broad generalizations, many researchers have concluded that indirectness is superior, and Bennett's work supports the effectiveness of formal styles. But the work of Powell (134), Flanders (48), and Soar (154) suggests that broad generalizations are inappropriate; that the effectiveness of a particular style depends on time factors, the flexibility of the teacher, and the nature of the learning tasks. In addition, Bennett's study suggests that using teachers' verbal behavior alone to indicate style results in oversimplified conclusions. A teacher's style involves many different variables which may manifest themselves through a variety of classroom activities. Thus, it appears safe to say that the problem of determining teaching effectiveness is more complex than first thought to be the case. Accordingly, let us turn our attention to the research findings on specific components of different teaching styles and strategies, beginning with feedback.

FEEDBACK

Reinforcement is a key concept in learning theory. The importance of positive and negative reinforcers to learning in lower animals is fairly well established, but the impact of different reinforcers on human learning is less clear. Educational theorists, almost universally, advocate the value of positive reinforcers in promoting pupil academic learning. However, the empirical evidence suggests some qualifications in applying this principle. For instance, many of us well remember being told that we should "always find something good to say about a student's paper." Presumably, positive comments encourage future learning, and there is research to support this claim. Working with second and third grades,

Brophy and Evertson (23, p. 94) found that "the use of symbolic rewards, particularly gold stars and smiling faces placed upon papers to be taken home and shown to the parents, or placed on charts in the room, showed consistent positive association with learning gains." Older students, on the other hand, may need more than symbolic rewards. Stewart and White (164), studying the effects of teacher comments and letter grades, suggested that "it is not the comment itself but the comment in conjunction with a letter grade which would be more likely to improve student performance." For secondary students, Page (128) found that a letter grade and a general comment were more effective in promoting subsequent learning than either a letter grade and a specific positive comment of the praise-or-encourage type or simply a letter grade without a comment. Thus, positive reinforcers in the form of written comments are valuable, but the nature of the comments and certain pupil characteristics may influence their overall effectiveness. Furthermore, the same qualifications appear to apply for verbal feedback.

Teacher verbal feedback takes many forms. Zahorik (189) identified 150 different types of feedback used in fifteen classes of third and sixth graders. Reanalysis of the data led him to collapse the 150 types into sixteen general categories with a majority of teacher comments falling into categories characterized as providing positive answers, simple praise and confirmation, and what Flanders (48) would label accepting or using student ideas.

How are these categories of verbal feedback employed by teachers in classroom interactions? Clearly, the type and extent of feedback will vary with the instructional activity, and, according to Zahorik (191), with different segments of the lesson. What is surprising is the small amount of classroom time during which teachers engage in the three categories of feedback. Referring to Zahorik's (190) work again, when teachers were asked what verbal behaviors they valued most highly, a large majority listed praise, both simple and elaborate, giving clear directions, and asking students to develop their ideas. However, classroom observations consistently indicate that these activities account for less than ten percent each of classroom interactions (2, 48, 54, 133, 168). Teachers in the early grades give more praise feedback than their colleagues in upper grades (191), and the existence of conflicting evidence suggests that teachers use pupil ideas and provide praise equally for males and females (24, 25, 42, 113) and for students of different socioeconomic backgrounds (2, 24, 60) and academic ability (25, 39, 60, 95).

The Effects of Praise

A few researchers have found correlations between teacher praise and pupil gains—correlations for samples of preschool children (53), disadvantaged children in kindergarten and first grade (156), and various samples of third through seventh grade students (48, 132, 188). Conversely, several investigators have found verbal praise to be unrelated to pupil progress. As examples, it is unrelated to achievement for first (47, 70) and second graders (69, 132), for upper elementary grade students (158, 177), and for middle school students (48). Evidence of the effects of praise on secondary students is missing and appears, as yet, to be an uncharted area of inquiry. But, as is apparent, the effects of praise on younger adolescents are unclear.

Why do we find discrepancies in the evidence? At first glance, one might conclude that praise must be unrelated to pupil learning or that our research techniques are not precise enough to measure its effects. Looking first at the research methodologies, there is some evidence to warrant the conclusion. The number of different definitions of praise used in studies is approximately equal to the number of studies conducted. Additionally, Samph (144) found that the presence of an observer in the classroom tends to modify the teacher's behavior. In his study, the observer's presence coincided with increases in teacher praise, questioning behavior, and the acceptance of student ideas.

Given these research limitations, the important question becomes, Must we accept the alternative hypothesis, that is, that praise is unrelated to academic achievement? Fortunately, recent research permits us to qualify our answer. Elaborate praise is unrelated to student gains (40), but Wallen (177) and Wright and Nuthall (188) found that minimal types of positive feedback correlated with achievement. Words like "Right," "Okay," "Good," "Uh-huh," and "Thank you" correlated with achievement gains for elementary-age students.

A second group of studies also sheds light on the effectiveness of praise. Praise directly related to an academic topic correlates with pupil progress (160), as does positive feedback when it is interpreted by the pupil as approval of his/her ideas or academic planning (158). However, to be effective, the praise must be teacher-initiated and sincere. Referring to his observations of 150 classrooms in 67 different schools, Goodlad (62) writes, "It seemed to us . . . that praise and verbal rewards (positive reinforcement) often were perfunctorily given and not clearly designed to attract a child's attention to the close relationships between his efforts and some goal or model." But if the praise is given sincerely, it can have a positive effect. For instance, Boak (22) found that junior high school students who rated their teachers "genuine" gained more than those students who gave their teachers lower "genuineness" marks.

The importance of giving genuine feedback that is academically related is supported by Brophy and Evertson's findings for teacher-initiated versus pupil-initiated interactions (23). Teacher-initiated praise correlated positively with student learning gains while praise occurring in pupil-initiated private interactions was negatively correlated with gains. In explaining this phenomenon, Brophy and Evertson write:

> . . . our observers believed that teacher praise in student-initiated situations tended to be brief, perfunctory, and generally lacking in both affect and specificity. In contrast, praise occurring in teacher-initiated interactions tended to be more specific (the teacher indicated in some detail what it was about the student's work that was praiseworthy, as opposed to giving the student a perfunctory "That's good"), and it tended to be delivered in a manner that suggested more credibility and positive affect. (23, p. 91)

The Brophy and Evertson study is important for the additional reason that it provides fairly conclusive evidence of the effects of praise on young children of different socioeconomic backgrounds and academic ability. These researchers conducted a large-scale field observation study of second and third grade teachers and their students over a two-year period. Generally, they found that praise was not nearly as positively related to learning gains as found in many earlier studies. More importantly, the findings revealed only a weak positive relationship between teacher praise and the achievement of low socioeconomic status children and a tendency for praise to be negatively related to achievement in high socioeconomic status children. Brophy and Evertson suggest that an explanation for these findings may lie in child development research. Weiner and Kukla (180) discovered a relationship between achievement motivation and the effects of praise and criticism. Students with high achievement motivation and records of academic success respond better to criticism than praise, while those with low achievement motivation and records of academic failure respond better to praise. Brophy and Evertson believe their high socioeconomic students exhibited high achievement motivation and that their low socioeconomic students exhibited low achievement motivation. Given this premise, they conclude:

> . . . a student who is accustomed to success, expects success, and is capable of achieving success with reasonable effort tends to respond well, at least in terms of improved achievement, to chiding criticism for failure that results from lack of effort or persistent application of skills. In contrast, the student who is accustomed to failure, expects failure, and has difficulty mastering something even if he persists long and hard is much more likely to be positively affected by encouragement and praise, and more likely to be negatively affected by criticism. (23, pp. 91-92)

In summary, then, elaborate teacher praise is not effective in promoting greater student achievement. Simple praise is effective, especially if it is related to the academic task at hand. Superficial attempts at praise are ineffective, while credible and genuine praise enhances achievement. Teacher-initiated praise is more meaningful than pupil-initiated praise. 19

Lastly, praising behavior may enhance greater gains for low socioeconomic and academic ability students, while mild criticism is more effective with high socioeconomic and academic ability students.

The Effects of Criticism

Interspersed through the studies of teacher praise are the research findings for the effect of teacher criticism on pupil learning. Teacher criticism accounts for less than ten percent of the total classroom interactions (2, 48, 168), and it appears to be indiscriminately directed at both males and females (42). Criticism is used more often in the primary grades (81), while social studies classes exhibited less teacher criticism than other classes (60, 81). Generally, research indicates that the use of criticism is unrelated to students' socioeconomic status, but at least one researcher found that lower achieving students received a greater amount of teacher criticism (60).

As discussed earlier, mild criticism may be related to achievement in high socioeconomic and academic ability students, but extreme criticism correlates negatively with student gains under all circumstances. For instance, investigators have found that extreme criticism relates negatively with achievement for disadvantaged children (69, 83), upper-middle-class students (132), and upper-middle-class students with above-average academic ability (158). On the other hand, two of these researchers found evidence supporting the use of mild criticism. Nonacceptance by the teacher for an incorrect pupil response, a form of mild criticism, was effective in promoting student gains (132), and disapproval both by commanding conformance and by eliciting clarification in a nonthreatening way was related to positive gains in reading (158).

Potentially, the most significant findings for the effects of teacher criticism on pupil progress is Soar's work with elementary children (152, 154). Paralleling his findings for teacher indirectness, Soar established a curvilinear relationships between criticism and pupil growth. In other words, there is an optimum level of criticism, a point at which greater pupil growth is maximized; beyond that point, greater criticism hinders progress. The optimum point depends upon the nature of the learning task. The learning of complex-abstract cognitive tasks occurs best in situations where teacher criticism is low; whereas the learning of less complex tasks and simple-concrete tasks is best mastered in situations involving varying degrees of criticism. In no case does extreme criticism enhance learning.

To summarize, strong disapproval and criticism, like elaborate praise, are not effective in promoting academic achievement. Mild criticism does correlate with achievement; its effectiveness, in large measure, depends upon the nature of the learning task. To quote Rosenshine:

. . . there is no evidence to support a claim that a teacher should avoid
telling a pupil that he is wrong, or should avoid giving him academic
directions. However, teachers who use a good deal of criticism appear
consistently to have classes which achieve less in most subject areas.
(140)

The Use of Pupil Ideas

Another major type of verbal feedback is teacher acceptance and use
of pupil ideas. As originally developed by Flanders, this type of feedback
can be subdivided into five subcategories:

1. *Acknowledging* the pupil's idea by repeating the nouns and logical
   contentions he/she has expressed;
2. *Modifying,* rephrasing, or conceptualizing it in the teacher's own
   words;
3. *Applying* the idea by using it to reach an inference or to take the
   next step in a logical analysis of a problem;
4. *Comparing* the ideas by drawing a relationship between the pupil's
   idea and one expressed earlier by either a pupil or a teacher;
5. *Summarizing* what was said by a pupil or a group of pupils. (48)

Unfortunately, to date too few studies have explored the effectiveness
of the use of student ideas on subsequent learning. Those that have
explored the area indicate this teaching strategy is beneficial. Fortune
(53), Morrison (121), and Perkins (132) all found positive correlations
between teachers' use of pupil ideas and the arithmetic, language arts, and
social studies achievements of fourth, fifth, and sixth graders. Flanders,
in reporting his findings based on fourth grade and sixth through eighth
grade classrooms, states, ". . . when classroom interaction patterns
indicate that pupils have opportunities to express their ideas, and when
these ideas are incorporated into the learning activities, then the pupils
seem to learn more and to develop more positive attitudes toward the
teacher and the learning activities" (48). The only exception to this
pattern of findings for elementary and middle-school-age students is
Fortune's study of preschool children (52). The age of the children and
the length of the learning sessions (five to seven minutes) may, however,
explain his results. Thus, the strategy of using pupil ideas *may* be
effective in encouraging pupil academic growth. More substantial conclusions must await further research findings.

THE USE OF QUESTIONS

A teaching style often purported to increase pupil learning is that of
using questions. Educational theorists claim that teachers who increase

the number of questions they ask and who ask higher-order questions will be more effective. Available research evidence supports this claim only in part.

Several studies have shown that the frequency of asking questions does correlate with achievement. Harris (69) and Wallen (177) have established that teachers' use of more questions with early elementary children (grades 1-3) was associated with increased academic growth. Seventh and eighth graders also appear to learn more (49), and interspersing questions throughout a high school science lesson is more effective than instructional lessons which lack opportunities for students to respond to questions (142).

Knowing that the frequency of questions correlates positively with achievement, one might ask if the pattern of questioning or the teacher's responses to pupils' answers influence achievement. Two experimental studies have explored the effects of different patterns of questioning (80, 126). In both studies, students were assigned to one of three treatment groups in which teachers (1) randomly asked questions around the classroom; (2) systematically asked questions according to a predetermined pattern; or (3) addressed questions only to those students who volunteered. No significant differences were found among the achievement levels of the three groups, although some differences were found for science achievement of males (80). The general conclusion, however, was that different questioning patterns do not influence achievement.

Research findings on teachers' responses to student answers are mixed. Wright and Nuthall (188) and Fortune (53) have found that repeating a student's correct response is related positively to learning. In addition, the Wright and Nuthall study is one of three (188, 152, 158) in which significant positive results were found for "probing" behavior. Probing refers to the teaching strategy of encouraging a student to elaborate upon his/her response or asking another question of the same student. On the other hand, Brophy and Evertson (23) found no relationship between seeking improved responses and achievement, and Gall et al. (55) were unable to discover substantial and consistent support for probing or redirecting behaviors. These mixed findings thus suggest that further study of this teacher strategy is warranted and necessary.

The search for the most effective type of question to be used in instruction has also produced mixed results. Part of the problem lies with the various definitions used by different researchers including those which distinguish between convergent and divergent questions (35), form and meaningful questions (69, 70), factual and process questions (158), open-ended and closed-ended questions (158), and many more (27, 75, 82, 83, 146). Use of such varying definitions makes comparisons between findings difficult. Recognizing the problem, we can conclude that at best the results are mixed; at worst, there are no significant differences. In response to the worst case, Rosenshine says:

> These non-significant results are puzzling. One would expect that the frequency of questions that encourage pupils "to seek explanations, to reason, to solve problems" (Perkins 1965) or the frequency of questions related to interpretation (Harris and Serwer 1966; Harris et al. 1968) would be consistently related to achievement. Yet these non-significant results have been experimentally replicated. (140)

Hutchinson (85) in his experimental study found that the creativity test scores of seventh graders increased with the presence of convergent questions, but their achievement test scores were almost identical. Miller (115), in a similar study, found no significant differences for mastery of facts or mastery of higher-order understandings.

Evidence which may explain why the results are mixed comes from the studies of Soar (152), Thompson and Bowers (167), and Furst (54). All three studies examined the impact of classroom interactions which included various mixes of higher-order and lower-order questions. Results indicated that the most effective pattern is a mixed one; therefore the relationship between levels of questions and achievement is once again curvilinear.

In summary, teaching styles that include questioning behaviors are effective. Increasing the number of questions used in instruction does correlate positively with achievement, while no particular pattern of asking questions around the classroom is most effective. Reinforcing student responses through repetition of correct answers and probing strategies may enhance learning. Finally, mixing factual questions and higher-order questions together through the instructional activity will produce more effective results than using either type alone.

STRUCTURING ACTIVITIES

Structuring activities are the presentation of instructional frameworks and/or teacher comments which are designed to assist the learner in identifying and focusing his/her attention on the content to be learned. Examples of instructional frameworks include pretests, behavioral objectives, and advance organizers. Teacher comments include statements which provide content-relevant information prior to a question, the use of definitions and examples, and the frequent mention and review of important points or main ideas. Structuring activities such as these have long been considered effective strategies for promoting learning. Only recently have investigators begun to test this assumption empirically.

Fortune (53), studying secondary English, mathematics, and social studies student teachers, discovered that the most effective teachers in terms of pupil gains used introductions to lessons, periodic reviews, and repetition of major points throughout the instructional units. Wright and Nuthall (188) found that providing content-relevant information prior to beginning a lesson was not related to pupil gains, but that providing this information at the end of the lesson was effective. Furthermore, acquisition of concepts improves when students are given additional concept-relevant material (9). Students of teachers who present concept definitions and examples achieve more than those not given this material, and presenting definitions plus three different sets of examples significantly improves learning (93).

Turning to instructional frameworks, the effects of using pretests appear to be mixed. For instance, Campbell and Stanley (28) and Welch and Walberg (181) cite eleven studies in which effects were indiscernible and three in which effects were discernible. Hartley and Davies (74) cite several more examples in each category (8, 65, 72, 103, 129). The best summary of the research findings in this area is provided by Hartley (73). In part, he concludes that pretests are most effective if (1) the instructional period following the pretest is short in duration, (2) they are used with more mature learners or students of higher academic ability, and (3) students understand the questions and know something about the material on the pretest.

The effectiveness of behavioral objectives in improving academic learning has been demonstrated in several studies (34, 97, 124, 143). As an example, Dalis (41) explored the effects of specific objectives, vague objectives, and paragraphs of information on the achievement of tenth grade health and safety students. Those who were provided specific objectives scored significantly better than those provided paragraphs or vague objectives. All the research, however, does not support the findings of Dalis and others. Studies by Bishop (21), Cook (36), DeRose (43), and Oswald (127) have found objectives to be unrelated to student achievement. After reviewing much of the pro and con evidence, Melton concludes that using behavioral objectives may be *in*effective—

1. If students ignore the objectives provided, either because they are unaware of them, or because prior experience suggests that it is not important to take note of them.
2. If the objectives are too general, or too ambiguous, to be of particular assistance.
3. If the objectives are of extreme facility or difficulty.
4. If the objectives of particular interest are only a small proportion of those provided to students.
5. If students are so conscientious, or so highly motivated, that they achieve the objectives regardless of whether or not they are specified. (112)

Stated positively. Melton's conclusions suggest that behavioral objectives will be effective if students see their importance, if they are specific, clear, and understandable, and if they are relevant to content.

Advance organizers are instructional frameworks designed to clarify the learning task ahead for the student. Ausubel (11), the originator of advance organizers, defines them as introductory material written at "a higher level of abstraction, generality, and inclusiveness than the learning itself" (12). For Ausubel, an organizer provides the learner with a subsumer which

1. gives him a general overview of the more detailed material in advance of his actual confrontation with it; and
2. provides organizing elements that are inclusive of and take into account most relevantly and efficiently both the particular content contained in the material and relevant concepts in cognitive structure. (12)

Although Ausubel (11) contends that he has provided clear criteria for constructing advance organizers, few researchers agree. Accordingly, studies reflect a multitude of operational definitions, and, as might be anticipated, the research findings show mixed results for their effectiveness in promoting learning. Grotelueschen and Sjogren (64) and Neisworth (125) have found that the achievement of above-average-ability students improves with the use of this instructional framework. Allen (1) concluded that organizers enhanced learning for above-average ninth grade social studies students, but not for less able students. Lawton (99,100), working with a sample of six- and ten-year-olds, found that advance organizers accelerated their movement from a preoperations level to the concrete operations level of learning.

On the other side of the coin, researchers such as Thelen (165), Clawson and Barnes (30), Pelletti (130), Shmurak (149), and Graben et al. (63) report nonsignificant effects for the use of advance organizers. Additionally, two investigators (26,104) found no significant difference in the achievement of students given visual or written organizers, and Jerrolds (87) reports that the presence or absence of organizers, or modified ones, is unrelated to the achievement of ninth grade students. Findings such as these, coupled with the significant findings noted, prompted Hartley and Davies (74) to quote one researcher as saying, "If it works, it's an advance organizer; if it doesn't work, it isn't." This may be an unfair judgment, but it points up the problem. Again, we must reserve formulating conclusions concerning the effectiveness of advance organizers until we obtain more conclusive evidence.

Summarizing the research on the effectiveness of teaching styles which include structuring activities, then, we find that introductory comments by teachers, reviews, and the presentation of content-relevant information are effective in promoting learning. Pretests and behavioral objectives may be effective depending upon such factors as design, relevancy to the learning task, and the abilities of students. The value of advance organizers is still open to question and study.

CLARITY OF PRESENTATION

A variable closely associated with the use of structuring comments is that of clarity of instruction. Researchers define this variable differently, but, in essence, it means presentation by the teacher in a clear fashion of the cognitive material to be mastered. Several studies have revealed that clarity of presentation is effective in promoting learning. Using low- and high-inference observation instruments, Good and Grouws (61) established that more effective teachers introduced and explained material more clearly than did less effective teachers. Belgard, Rosenshine, and Gage (17), using a similar research design, obtained similar results. After each fifteen-minute lecture on three consecutive days of instruction, twelfth grade social studies students were asked to rate teacher effectiveness on several variables. Classes of students who gave their teachers high marks for clarity of aims and of presentation achieved more than classes who gave their teachers low marks on these variables. Furthermore, Hiller, Fisher, and Kaess (77) found that classes in which teachers used fewer vague words such as "some," "many," "of course," and "a little" registered greater gains than classes where these words were frequently used. Finally, Wright and Nuthall (188) report that effective third grade teachers were those who phrased their questions so that they were answered the first time and did not have to supply additional information before students could give the desired response. The single study reviewed by the author that did not report a strong relationship between teacher clarity and achievement is Brophy and Evertson's work with second and third graders. These researchers explain their results as follows:

> Perhaps the complexity levels of the material taught at these grade levels is low enough that clarity is not a major consideration, as much as it is for teaching certain subjcts at higher grade levels, particularly difficult subjects with much abstract content. In general, it seems reasonable to suppose that teacher clarity becomes increasingly important as the curriculum becomes more complex. (23, p. 82)

Another way of looking at clarity of presentation is to consider perceptions about lesson and class organization. Presumably if presentations are clear, students should perceive the organization of the lesson. Results from the Belgard, Rosenshine, and Gage (17) study cited confirm this hypothesis. In addition to high marks on clarity, effective teachers were rated high on organization of lesson. Lawrenz (98) found that classes where students perceived the goals of instruction achieved more than classes where students were unable to identify such goals. And in several studies, Anderson and Walberg (5, 6, 173, 175) have found a negative relationship between perceived class disorganization and achievement. In other words, students who, as a group, perceived their classes as disorganized achieved less than those who rated their classes high on organization. Thus, it is apparent that effective teaching styles include teacher behaviors which promote clarity of presentation.

TASK-ORIENTED TEACHING STYLES

Several researchers have attempted to determine the effects of task-oriented behavior on academic achievement. In the eyes of many educators "time on task" should be related to achievement. Research findings indicate that it is a positive relationship. Three studies (23, 153, 160) have shown that time spent directly on instruction is significantly related to achievement for low socioeconomic status children. In addition, Spaulding (158) found that teachers who were rated more businesslike and orderly were more effective in promoting achievement, and Fortune (53) and Kleinman (94) report significant achievement results were obtained in those classes that were taught by more businesslike (responsible, steady, systematic, poised) teachers. It is apparent from these studies that task-oriented behavior correlates positively with pupil learning and consequently warrants being viewed as part of an effective teaching style.

ENTHUSIASTIC TEACHING

A teaching behavior viewed desirable, almost universally, is teacher enthusiasm. Its effectiveness in promoting pupil achievement is supported by a considerable body of research evidence. Roberts and Becker (136) report that the variables of teacher dynamism and teacher delivery distinguish effective from ineffective teachers. Wallen (177, 178) reports that the teacher variable "stimulating" was significantly correlated with arithmetic achievement for first and third graders, and with reading achievement for sixty-five classes of first through fifth graders. Fortune (53) asked social studies, mathematics, and English student teachers in their field experience to teach short lessons to fourth, fifth, and sixth grade classes. Using supervisor ratings, he found that the pupils of student teachers who were rated more stimulating scored higher on achievement measures. In an experimental study, Mastin (107) manipulated teacher enthusiasm by having twenty teachers present one lecture with enthusiasm and one lecture with indifference to their sixth and seventh grade classes. Class average achievement scores for the lessons taught with enthusiasm were higher for nineteen of the twenty classes.

Research on animation and speech patterns also supports the effectiveness of teacher enthusiasm. Rosenshine (137) reports that Jersild (88) and Ehrensberger (46) experimentally manipulated teachers' hand gestures and found significant retention levels for the content that was accompanied by gestures. Gauger (58) found similar results in an experiment with high school students. In an interesting study of speech inflection, McCoard (122) concluded that pitch and volume, and the variations in each, correlate with achievement.

The one important piece of research that reports a lack of relationship between enthusiasm and pupil gains is the study by Brophy and Evertson (23). This study is important because its results tend to contradict the assumption that teacher enthusiasm is essential to learning in young children. Brophy and Evertson recognize that their findings may be biased by characteristics of their teacher sample and the research methodology, but they also suggest

> ... that an argument can be made that they [affect and enthusiasm] are less important with younger children than with older children; despite the acknowledged importance of adults relative to the peer group for younger children. For one thing, young children tend to accept without much questioning or opposition the idea that they are supposed to go to school and "learn," and that the teacher's job is to teach them. . . . younger children tend to accept the school curriculum as given, so that enthusiasm and some of the other teacher characteristics that are important in generating interest in a subject area among older students are superfluous with younger ones. Thus, it can be argued that affect, enthusiasm, and related teacher characteristics are less important with young children, particularly those in high SES schools, than they are with older children and adolescents. (23, p. 106)

Teacher enthusiasm, then, is a significant correlate of pupil achievement. Stimulating teaching effectively promotes student learning gains. Its presence is important for academic learning at all age levels, but especially for older adolescents.

CLASSROOM REWARD STRUCTURES

A topic that has received a considerable amount of attention in recent years is classroom reward structures. In large part, teaching styles and strategies determine the type of reward structure present in the classroom. Michaels identifies four basic structures that may be present as follows:

1. individual reward contingencies, where performance is rewarded according to predetermined standards for each individual;
2. group reward contingencies, where performance is rewarded according to predetermined standards for each group, and rewards are distributed equally among group members;
3. individual competition, where rewards are dependent upon the relative performance of other individuals;

4. group competition, where group rewards are dependent upon the relative performance of other groups. (114)

Typically, individual competition or individual reward contingencies has been the predominate structure present in classrooms. Increasingly, these structures have been criticized as being less effective than others in promoting academic learning.

Which reward structure produces the greatest pupil achievement? The research evidence favors the use of individual competition. As examples, Clifford (32) found that individual competition structures were more effective than individual reward contingencies in teaching digit-letter substitutions to fifth and sixth grade students. Maller (105) found that individual competition produces greater mathematics achievement scores than does group competition in fifth through eighth graders. These and other studies (67, 147, 185) indicate that individual competition structures result in greater pupil gains. This conclusion merits at least two qualifications, however. The research of Miller and Hamblin (116) suggests that the effectiveness of a particular reward structure depends, in part, upon the structure of the learning task. In other words, if the task is an interdependent one, i.e., it could not be performed by an individual, group reward contingencies are more positively related to achievement than competitive structures.

A second qualification reflects the focus of this publication. We are concerned here only with academic achievement. Group process skills may be achieved more effectively through group reward structures, and in fact, this claim has been substantiated by investigators such as Coleman (33), Bronfenbrenner (26), and Johnson and Johnson (91). Equally important, studies by Hamblin et al. (67) and Edwards et al. (45) have shown that both academic and group process goals can be achieved when individual and group reward structures are used concurrently in the classroom.

STUDENT PERCEPTIONS OF CLASSROOM CLIMATE

A final way of looking at the effects of different teaching styles on pupil learning is to consider studies on student perceptions of the classroom environment. Partial results from such studies have been used in the preceding pages to document research findings, but additional results deserve brief attention. Moos and Moos (120) found that achievement was greater for classes that students rated high in involvement and affiliation. They also found greater achievement related to the extent to which students pay attention and show interest and come to know and work with their peers. Anderson (5), Walberg (173), and Walberg and Anderson (175) report a positive relationship between cognitive learning and those classes students perceive as cohesive (the presence of peer friendships), satisfying (students enjoy their class work), environmentally rich (necessary books and materials are readily available), and difficult (students are constantly challenged). Conversely, these same researchers report negative relationships between achievement and those classes perceived as exhibiting student apathy, friction, cliquishness, and favoritism. Thus, the results suggest that teaching styles and strategies which challenge students to do their best and which encourage group membership and cohesiveness will be particularly effective in promoting pupil achievement.

CONCLUDING COMMENT

In closing, it seems appropriate once again to caution the reader in interpreting the information presented in this publication. Teaching is a complex act, and effective teaching involves a multitude of variables. This fact, coupled with the limitations of our present research methodologies, hinders identification of precise cause-and-effect relationships. To date, an overwhelming amount of the research has been able to establish only correlational relationships between selected teaching styles and behaviors and pupil achievement. Establishing these relationships is an example of the contributions that research can make to improving classroom teaching, but we must not settle for these results alone. Additional research is urgently needed. In the interim period, the author hopes the information provided in the foregoing pages will assist teachers in identifying effective teaching strategies that can be used in classroom instruction.

SELECTED REFERENCES

1. Allen, D. I. "Some Effects of Advance Organizers and Level of Questions on the Learning and Retention of Written Social Studies Material." *Journal of Educational Psychology* 61:333–39; 1970.
2. Altman, H. "Teacher-Student Interaction in Inner-City and Advantaged Classes Using the Science Curriculum Improvement Study." *Classroom Interaction Newsletter* 6:5–16; 1970.
3. Amidon, E. J., and Flanders, N. A. *The Role of the Teacher in the Classroom.* Minneapolis: Amidon, 1963.
4. ———, and Hough, J. B., eds. *Interaction Analysis: Theory, Research and Application.* Reading, Mass.: Addison-Wesley, 1967.
5. Anderson, G. J. "Effects of Classroom Social Climate on Individual Learning." *American Educational Research Journal* 7:135–52; 1970.
6. ———, and Walberg, H. J. "Classroom Climate and Group Learning." *International Journal of the Educational Sciences* 2:175–80; 1968.
7. Anderson, H. H. "The Measurement of Domination and of Socially Integrative Behavior in Teachers' Contacts with Children." *Child Development* 10:73–89; 1939.
8. Apter, M. J., et al. "A Comparison of the Multiple-Choice and Constructed Response Pre-Tests in Programmed Instruction." *Programmed Learning and Educational Technology* 2:125-30; 1971.
9. Armento, B. J. "Teachers' Behaviors Related to Student Achievement on a Social Science Concept Test." *Journal of Teacher Education* 28:46–52; 1977.
10. Arrington, R. E. "Time-Sampling Studies of Child Behavior." *Psychological Monographs* 51:4; 1939.
11. Ausubel, D. P. "In Defense of Advance Organizers: A Reply to the Critics." *Review of Educational Research* 48:251–57; 1978.
12. ———. *The Psychology of Meaningful Verbal Learning.* New York: Grune and Stratton, 1963.
13. Averch, H. S., et al. *How Effective is Schooling?* Englewood Cliffs, N.J.: Educational Technology Publications, 1974.
14. Barnes, B. R., and Clawson, E. U. "Do Advance Organizers Facilitate Learning? Recommendations for Further Research Based on an Analysis of 32 Studies." *Review of Educational Research* 45:637–59; 1975.
15. Barr, A. S. *Characteristic Differences in the Teaching Performance of Good and Poor Teachers of the Social Studies.* Bloomington, Ill: Public School Publishing, 1929.
16. Barron, R. R. *The Effects of Advanced Organizers upon the Reception, Learning and Retention of General Science Content.* HEW Project 18-030 Final Report. New York: Syracuse University, 1971.
17. Belgard, M.; Rosenshine, B.; and Gage, N. L. "The Teacher's Effectiveness in Explaining: Evidence on Its Generality and Correlation with Pupils' Ratings and Attention Scores." In *Research Into Classroom Processes,* edited by I. Westbury and A. A. Bellack, pp. 182–91. New York: Teachers College Press, Teachers College, Columbia University, 1971.
18. Bellack, A. A., ed. *Theory and Research in Teaching.* New York: Teachers College Press, Teachers College, Columbia University, 1963.
19. ———, et al. *The Language of the Classroom.* New York: Teachers College Press, Teachers College, Columbia University, 1966.

20. Bennett, N. *Teaching Styles and Pupil Progress*. Cambridge, Mass.: Harvard University Press, 1976.

21. Bishop, D. D. "Effectiveness of Prior Exposure to Performance Objectives as a Technique for Improvement of Student Recall and Retention." Doctoral dissertation, Ohio State University, 1969.

22. Boak, R. T. R., and Conklin, R. C. "The Effect of Teachers' Levels of Interpersonal Skills on Junior High School Students' Achievements and Anxiety." *American Educational Research Journal* 12:537–49; 1975.

23. Brophy, Jere E., and Evertson, Carolyn M. *Learning from Teaching: A Developmental Perspective*. Boston: Allyn and Bacon, 1976.

24. ———, et al. *Communication of Teacher Expectations: Fifth Grade*. Report Series No. 93. Austin: University of Texas, 1973.

25. ———, and Good, T. L. "Teachers' Communications of Differential Expectations for Children's Classroom Performance: Some Behavioral Data." *Journal of Educational Psychology* 61:365–74; 1970.

26. Bronfenbrenner, U. *Two Worlds of Childhood*. New York: Russell Sage Foundation, 1970.

27. Buggey, J. L. "A Study of the Relationship of Classroom Questions and Social Studies Achievement of Second Grade Children." Doctoral dissertation, University of Washington, 1971.

28. Campbell, D. T., and Stanley, J. C. "Experimental and Quasi-Experimental Designs for Research on Teaching." In *Handbook of Research on Teaching*, edited by N. L. Gage, pp. 171–247. Chicago: Rand McNally, 1963.

29. Campbell, J. R. "Cognitive and Affective Process Development and Its Relations to a Teacher's Interaction Ratio." *Journal of Research in Science Teaching* 8:317–23; 1971.

30. Clawson, E. U., and Barnes, B. R. "The Effects of Organizers on the Learning of Structured Anthropology Materials in Elementary Grades." *Journal of Experimental Education* 42:11–15; 1973.

31. Clifford, M. M. "Motivational Effects of Competition and Goal Setting in Reward and Non-Reward Conditions." *Journal of Experimental Education* 39:11–16, 1971.

32. ———. "Effects of Competition as a Motivational Technique in the Classroom." *American Educational Research Journal* 9:123–37; 1972.

33. Coleman, J. S. "Academic Achievement and the Structure of Competition." *Harvard Educational Review* 29:339–51; 1959.

34. Conlon, B. A. "A Comparison of the Performance of Seventh-Grade Students with and without Prior Knowledge of the Objectives of an Individualized Science Program." Doctoral dissertation, Florida State University, 1970.

35. Conners, C. K., and Eisenberg, L. *The Effects of Teacher Behavior on Verbal Intelligence in Operation Head Start Children*. Project No. 510, U.S. Office of Economic Opportunity. Baltimore: Johns Hopkins University, 1966.

36. Cook, J. M. *Learning and Retention by Informing Students of Behavioral Objectives and Their Place in the Hierarchical Learning Sequence*. U.S. Office of Education Final Report. College Park, Md.: University of Maryland, 1969.

37. Cook, R. E. "The Effect of Teacher Methodology upon Certain Achievements of Students in Secondary School Biology." Doctoral dissertation, University of Iowa, 1967.

38. Corey, S. M. "The Teachers Out-Talk the Pupils." *The School Review* 48:745–52; 1940.

39. Cornbleth, C., et al. "Teacher-Pupil Interaction and Teacher Expectations for Pupil Achievement in Secondary School Social Studies Classes." Paper presented at Annual Conference of American Educational Research Association, Chicago, 1972.

40. Crawford, J., et al. "Classroom Dyadic Interaction: Factor Structure of Process Variables and Achievement Correlates." *Journal of Educational Psychology* 69:761–72; 1977.

41. Dalis, G. T. "Effects of Precise Objectives upon Student Achievement in Health Education." *Journal of Experimental Education* 39:20–23; 1970.

42. Davis, D. L. Jr., and Slobodian, J. J. "Teacher Behavior Toward Boys and Girls During First Grade Reading Instruction." *American Educational Research Journal* 4:261–70; 1967.

43. DeRose, J. "Independent Study in High School Chemistry." *Journal of Chemical Education* 47:553–60; 1970.

44. Dunkin, M. J., and Biddle, B. J. *The Study of Teaching.* New York: Holt, Rinehart and Winston, 1974.

45. Edwards, K. J. et al. "Games and Teams: A Winning Combination." *Simulation and Games* 3:247–69; 1972.

46. Ehrensberger, R. "An Experimental Study of the Relative Effectiveness of Certain Forms of Emphasis in Public Speaking." *Speech Monographs* 12:94–111; 1945.

47. Felsenthal, H. *Sex Differences in Teacher-Pupil Interactions in First Grade Reading Instruction.* Paper presented at Annual Conference of American Educational Research Association, Minneapolis, 1970.

48. Flanders, N. A. *Analyzing Teacher Behavior.* Reading: Mass.: Addison-Wesley, 1970.

49. ———. "Some Relationships Among Teacher Influence, Pupil Attitudes and Achievement." In *Interaction Analysis: Theory, Research and Application,* edited by E. J. Amidon and J. B. Hough, pp. 217-42. Reading, Mass.: Addison-Wesley, 1967.

50. ———. "Teacher and Classroom Influences on Individual Learning." Paper presented at Annual Curriculum Research Institute, Association for Supervision and Curriculum Development, Washington, D.C., 1961.

51. ———. *Teacher Influences, Pupil Attitudes and Achievement.* Project No. 397, U.S. Office of Education. Ann Arbor, Mich.: University of Michigan, 1960.

52. Fortune, J. C. "The Generality of Presenting Behaviors in Teaching Preschool Children." Unpublished paper, 1966.

53. ———. *A Study of the Generalities of Presenting Behaviors in Teaching.* Project No. 6-8468, U.S. Office of Education. Memphis: Memphis State University, 1967.

54. Furst, N. F. "The Multiple Languages of the Classroom." Paper presented at Annual Conference of American Educational Research Association, New York, 1967.

55. Gall, M. D., et al. "Effects of Questioning Techniques and Recitation on Student Learning." *American Educational Research Journal* 15:175–99; 1978.

56. Gallagher, J. J.; Nuthall, G. A.; and Rosenshine, B. *Classroom Observation.* Chicago: Rand McNally and Co., 1970.

57. Gallup, G. H. "The 10th Annual Gallup Poll of the Public's Attitudes Toward the Public Schools." *Phi Delta Kappan* 160:33–45; 1978.

58. Gauger, P. W. "The Effect of Gesture and the Presence or Absence of the Speaker on the Listening Comprehension of Eleventh and Twelfth Grade

High School Pupils." Doctoral dissertation, University of Wisconsin, 1951.

59. Good, T. L.; Biddle, B. J.; and Brophy, J. E. *Teachers Make a Difference.* New York: Holt, Rinehart and Winston, 1975.

60. ———, et al. "Effects of Teacher Sex, Student Sex, and Student Achievement on Classroom Interaction." *Journal of Educational Psychology* 65:74–87; 1973.

61. ———, and Grouws, D. A. "Teaching Effects: A Process-Product Study in Fourth Grade Mathematics Classrooms." *Journal of Teacher Education* 28:49–54; 1977.

62. Goodlad, J. L.; Klein, M. F.; and Associates. *Looking Behind the Classroom Door.* Worthington, Ohio: Charles Jones Publishing, 1974.

63. Graben, R. A., et al. "The Effects of Subsuming Concepts on Student Achievement of Unfamiliar Science Learning Materials." *Journal of Research on Science Teaching* 9:277–79; 1972.

64. Grotelueschen, A. D., and Sjogren, D. O. "Effects of Differential Structural Introductory Materials and Learning Tasks on Learning Transfer." *American Educational Research Journal* 5:191–202; 1968.

65. Gustafson, H. W., and Toole, D. L. "Effects of Adjunct Questions, Pre-Testing, and Degree of Student Supervision on Learning from an Instructional Text." *Journal of Experimental Education* 39:53–58; 1970.

66. Halpin, A. W., and Croft, D. B. "The Organizational Climate of Schools." *Administrator's Notebook* 11:1–4; 1963.

67. Hamblin, R. L. et al. "Group Contingencies, Poor Tutoring and Accelerated Academic Achievement." In *A New Direction for Education: Behavior Analysis,* edited by E. Ramp and W. Hopkins, pp. 41–53. Lawrence, Kans.: University of Kansas, 1971.

68. Harnischfeger, A., and Wiley, D. E. "Achievement Test Scores Drop. So What?" *Educational Researcher* 5:5–12; 1976.

69. Harris, A. J., et al. *A Continuation of the CRAFT Project: Comparing Reading Approaches with Disadvantaged Urban Negro Children in Primary Grades.* Project No. 5-0570, U.S. Office of Education. New York: City University of New York, 1968.

70. ———, and Serwer, B. *Comparison of Reading Approaches in First Grade Teaching with Disadvantaged Children: The CRAFT Project.* Project No. 2677, U.S. Office of Education. New York: City University of New York, 1966.

71. Hart, F. W. *Teachers and Teaching: By Ten Thousand High School Seniors.* New York: Macmillan, 1936.

72. Hartley, J. "Observations on the Training Function of a Pre-Test." *Industrial Training International* 4:134; 1969.

73. ———. "The Effects of Pre-Testing on Post-Test Performance." *Instructional Science* 2:193–214; 1973.

74. ———, and Davies, I. K. "Preinstructional Strategies: The Role of Pretests, Behavioral Objectives, Overviews and Advance Organizers." *Review of Educational Research* 46:239–65; 1976.

75. Hearn, D. D. "The Effects of Questions in Facilitating Fourth Grade Pupils' Acquisition of Information from Printed Instructional Materials in the Social Studies." Doctoral dissertation, University of Texas, 1969.

76. Herman, W. L., Jr., "An Analysis of the Activities and Verbal Behavior of Selected Fifth Grade Social Studies Classes." *Classroom Interaction Newsletter* 2:27–29; 1967.

77. Hiller, J. H.; Fisher, G. A.; and Kaess, W. "A Computer Investigation of

Verbal Characteristics of Effective Classroom Learning." *American Educational Research Journal* 6:661–77; 1969.

78. Hoehn, A. J. "A Study of Social Status Differentiation in the Classroom Behavior of Nineteen Third Grade Teachers." *Journal of Social Psychology* 39:269–92; 1954.

79. Hoetker, J., and Ahlbrand, W. P., Jr. "The Persistence of Recitation." *American Educational Research Journal* 6:145–67; 1969.

80. Hughes, D. C. "An Experimental Investigation of the Effects of Pupil Responding and Teacher Reacting on Pupil Achievement." *American Educational Research Journal* 10:21–37; 1973.

81. Hughes, M. M. *Assessment of the Quality of Teaching in Elementary Schools.* Salt Lake City: University of Utah Press, 1959.

82. Hunkins, F. P. "The Effects of Analysis and Evaluation Questions on Various Levels of Achievement." *Journal of Experimental Education* 38:45–58; 1969.

83. ———, et al. *Review of Research in Social Studies Education: 1970–1975.* Boulder, Colorado: ERIC Clearinghouse for Social Studies/Social Science Education, 1977.

84. Hunter, C. P. "Classroom Climate and Pupil Characteristics in Special Classes for the Educationally Handicapped." Doctoral dissertation, University of Southern California, 1968.

85. Hutchinson, W. L. "Creative and Productive Thinking in the Classroom." Doctoral dissertation, University of Utah, 1963.

86. Hyman, R. T. *Ways of Teaching.* Philadelphia: J. B. Lippincott Co. 1970.

87. Jerrolds, B. W. "The Effects of Advance Organizers in Reading for the Retention of Specific Facts." Doctoral dissertation, University of Wisconsin, 1967.

88. Jersild, A. T. "Modes of Emphasis in Public Speaking." *Journal of Applied Psychology* 12:611–20; 1928.

89. ———, and Meige, M. F. "Direct Observation as a Research Method." *Review of Educational Research* 9:1939.

90. Johns, J. P. "The Relationship Between Teacher Behaviors and the Incidence of Thought-Provoking Questions by Students in Secondary Schools." *Journal of Educational Research* 62:117–22; 1968.

91. Johnson, D. W., and Johnson, R. T. "Instructional Goal Structure: Cooperative, Competitive, or Individualistic." *Review of Educational Research* 44:213–40; 1974.

92. Joyce, B., and Weil, M. *Models of Teaching.* Englewood Cliffs, N. J.: Prentice-Hall, 1972.

93. Klausmier, H. J., and Feldman, K. V. *The Effects of a Definition and a Varying Number of Examples and Non-Examples on Concept Attainment.* Technical Report No. 280. Madison, Wis.: Wisconsin Research and Development Center for Cognitive Learning, 1973.

94. Kleinman, G. "General Science Teachers' Questions, Pupil and Teacher Behaviors and Pupils' Understanding of Science." Doctoral dissertation, University of Virginia, 1964.

95. Kranz, P. L., et al. "The Relationships Between Teacher Perception of Pupils and Teacher Behavior Toward Those Pupils." Paper presented at Annual Conference of American Educational Research Association, Minneapolis, 1970.

96. Kratz, H. E. "Characteristics of the Best Teachers as Recognized by Children." *Pedagogical Seminary* 3:413–18; 1896.

97. Lawrence, R. M. "The Effects of Three Types of Organizing Devices on Academic Achievement." Doctoral dissertation, University of Maryland, 1970.

98. Lawrenz, F. "The Relationship Between Science Teacher Characteristics and Student Achievement and Attitude." *Journal of Research in Science Teaching* 12:433–37; 1975.

99. Lawton, J. T. "An Analytical Study of the Use of Advance Organizers in Facilitating Children's Learning." Doctoral dissertation, University of Leeds, England, 1974.

100. ———. "The Use of Advance Organizers in the Learning and Retention of Logical Operations and Social Studies Concepts." *American Educational Research Journal* 14:25–43; 1977.

101. ———, and Wanska, S. K. "Advance Organizers as a Teaching Strategy: A Reply to Barnes and Clawson." *Review of Educational Research* 47:233–44; 1977.

102. Lewin, K.; Lippitt, R.; and White, R. "Patterns of Aggressive Behavior in Experimentally Created 'Social Climates'." *Journal of Social Psychology* 10:271–99; 1939.

103. Lucas, A. M. "Inflated Post-Test Scores Seven Months After Pre-Test." *Science Education* 56:381–88; 1972.

104. Lucas, S. B. "The Effects of Utilizing Three Types of Advance Organizers for Learning a Biological Concept in Seventh Grade Science." Doctoral dissertation, Pennsylvania State University, 1972.

105. Maller, J. B. *Cooperation and Competition: An Experimental Study on Motivation.* New York: Teachers College, Columbia University, 1929.

106. Masling, J., and Stern, G. "Effect of the Observer in the Classroom." *Journal of Educational Psychology* 60:351–54; 1969.

107. Mastin, V. E. "Teacher Enthusiasm." *Journal of Educational Research* 56:385–86; 1963.

108. Measel, W., and Mood, D. W. "Teacher Verbal Behaviors and Teacher and Pupil Thinking in Elementary School." *Journal of Educational Research* 66:99–102; 1972.

109. Medley, D. M. "Early History of Research on Teacher Behavior." *International Review of Education* 18:430–38; 1972.

110. ———, and Mitzel, H. E. "A Technique for Measuring Classroom Behavior." *Journal of Educational Psychology* 49:86–92; 1958.

111. ———, and ———. "Some Behavioral Correlates of Teacher Effectiveness." *Journal of Educational Psychology* 50:239–46; 1959.

112. Melton, R. F. "Resolution of Conflicting Claims Concerning the Effect of Behavioral Objectives on Student Learning." *Review of Educational Research* 48:291–302; 1978.

113. Meyer, W. J., and Thompson, G. C. "Sex Differences in the Distribution of Teacher Approval and Disapproval Among Sixth Grade Children." *Journal of Educational Psychology* 47:385–96; 1956.

114. Michaels, J. W. "Classroom Reward Structures and Academic Performance." *Review of Educational Research* 47: 87–98; 1977.

115. Miller, G. L. "Collaborative Teaching and Pupil Thinking." *Journal of Teacher Education* 17:337–58; 1966.

116. Miller, L. K., and Hamblin, R. L. "Interdependence, Differential Rewarding, and Productivity." *American Sociological Review* 28:768–78; 1963.

117. Minuchin, P., et al. *The Psychological Import of School Experience.* New York: Basic Books, 1969.

118. Mitzel, H. E. "Teacher Effectiveness." In *Encyclopedia of Educational*

Research, edited by G. W. Harris, pp. 1481–86. 3d ed. New York: Macmillan, 1960.

119. Mohan, M., and Hull, R. E. *Teaching Effectiveness: Its Meaning, Assessment, and Improvement.* Englewood Cliffs, N. J.: Educational Technology Publications, 1975.

120. Moos, R. H., and Moos, B. S. "Classroom Social Climate and Student Absences and Grades." *Journal of Educational Psychology* 70:263–69; 1978.

121. Morrison, B. M. "The Reactions of Internal and External Children to Patterns of Teaching Behavior." Doctoral dissertation, University of Michigan, 1966.

122. McCoard, W. B. "Speech Factors as Related to Teaching Efficiency." *Speech Monographs* 11:53–64; 1944.

123. McKinney, J. D. "Relationship Between Classroom Behavior and Academic Achievement." *Journal of Educational Psychology* 67:198–203; 1975.

124. McNeil, J. D. "Concomitants of Using Behavioral Objectives in the Assessment of Teacher Effectiveness." *Journal of Experimental Education* 36:96–74; 1967.

125. Neisworth, J. T. "The Use of Advance Organizers with the Educable Mentally Retarded." Doctoral dissertation, University of Pittsburgh, 1967.

126. Nuthall, G., and Church, J. "Experimental Studies of Teaching Behavior." In *Towards a Science of Teaching,* edited by G. Chanan, pp. 9-25. Windsor. Berks: NFER Publishing, 1973.

127. Oswald, J. M. "Instructor Specified Instructional Objectives and Achievement of Social Studies Knowledge and Comprehension." Doctoral dissertation, Stanford University, 1970.

128. Page, E. B. "Teacher Comments and Student Performance: A Seventy-Four Classroom Experiment in School Motivation." *Journal of Educational Psychology* 49:173–81; 1958.

129. Peeck, J. "Effects of Pre-Test Questions on Delayed Retention of Prose Materials." *Journal of Educational Psychology* 61:241–46; 1970.

130. Pelletti, J. C. "The Effects of Graphic Roles on Learning Geography Materials in the Middle Grades." Doctoral dissertation, University of Georgia, 1973.

131. Penny, R. E., "Presentational Behaviors Related to Success in Teaching." Doctoral dissertation, Stanford University, 1969.

132. Perkins, H. V. "Classroom Behavior and Underachievement." *American Educational Research Journal* 2:1–12; 1965.

133. ———. "A Procedure for Assessing the Classroom Behavior of Students and Teachers." *American Educational Research Journal* 1:249–60; 1964.

134. Powell, E. R. "Teacher Behavior and Pupil Achievement." Paper presented at Annual Conference of American Educational Research Association, Chicago, 1968.

135. Rian, H. "Teacher Leadership and Pupil Reaction: The Authoritarian-Democratic Dimension Revisited." *Scandinavian Journal of Educational Research* 13:1–15; 1969.

136. Roberts, C. L., and Becker, S. L. "Communication and Teaching Effectiveness in Industrial Education." *American Educational Research Journal* 13:181–97; 1976.

137. Rosenshine, B. "Enthusiastic Teaching: A Research Review." *School Review* 78:499–515; 1970.

138. ———. "Recent Research on Teaching Behaviors and Student Achievement." *Journal of Teacher Education* 27:61–64; 1976.

139. ———. *Teaching Behaviors and Student Achievement.* Slough, England: National Foundation for Educational Research in England and Wales, 1971.

140. ———. "Teaching Behaviors Related to Pupil Achievement: A Review of Research." In *Research into Classroom Processes,* edited by I. Westbury and A. A. Bellack, pp. 51–98. New York: Teachers College, Columbia University, 1971.

141. ———, and Furst, N. "Research on Teacher Performance." In *Research in Teacher Education,* edited by B. Othanel Smith, pp. 37–72. Englewood Cliffs, N. J.: Prentice-Hall, 1971.

142. Rothkopf, E. Z., and Bloom, R. D. "Effects of Interpersonal Interaction on the Instructional Value of Adjunct Questions in Learning from Written Material." *Journal of Educational Psychology* 61:417–22; 1970.

143. ———, and Kaplan, R. "Exploration of the Effect of Density and Specificity of Instructional Objectives on Learning from Text." *Journal of Educational Psychology* 63:295–302; 1972.

144. Samph, T. "Observer Effects on Teacher Verbal Classroom Behavior." *Journal of Educational Psychology* 68: 736–41; 1977.

145. ———. "Teacher Behavior and the Reading Performance of Below-Average Achievers." *Journal of Educational Research* 67:268–70; 1974.

146. Savage, T. U., Jr. "A Study of the Relationship of Classroom Questions and Social Studies Achievement of Fifth Grade Children." Doctoral dissertation, University of Washington, 1972.

147. Scott, W. E., and Cherrington, D. J. "Effects of Competitive, Cooperative, and Individualistic Reinforcement Contingencies." *Journal of Personality and Social Psychology* 30:748–58; 1974.

148. Shavelson, R., and Dempsey-Atwood, N. "Generalizability of Measures of Teaching Behaviors." *Review of Educational Research* 46:553–611; 1976.

149. Shmurak, C. B. "The Effect of Varying the Cognitive Style of Advance Organizers on Learning of Expository Science Material by Eighth Graders." Doctoral dissertation, Indiana University, 1974.

150. Slavin, R. E. "Classroom Reward Structure: An Analytical and Practical Review." *Review of Educational Research* 47:633–50; 1977.

151. Snider, R. M. "A Project to Study the Nature of Effective Physics Training." Doctoral dissertation, Cornell University, 1966.

152. Soar, R. S. *An Integrative Approach to Classroom Learning.* Project Nos. 5-R11 MH01096 and 7R11 MH02045, National Institute of Mental Health. University of South Carolina and Temple University respectively, 1966.

153. ———. *Follow Through Classroom Process Measurement and Pupil Growth (1970–71): Final Report.* Gainesville: University of Florida, 1973.

154. ———. "Optimum Teacher-Pupil Interaction for Pupil Growth." *Educational Leadership* 26:275–80; 1968.

155. ———. "Teacher Behavior Related to Pupil Growth." *International Review of Education* 18:508–26; 1972.

156. ———, et al. "The Validation of an Observation System for Classroom Management." Paper presented at Annual Conference of American Educational Research Association, New York, 1971.

157. ———, and Soar, R. M. "An Attempt to Identify Measures of Teacher Effectiveness from Four Studies." *Journal of Teacher Education* 27:261–67; 1976.

158. Spaulding, R. L. *Achievement, Creativity, and Self-Concept Correlates of Teacher-Pupil Transactions in Elementary School Classrooms.* Project No. 1352, U.S. Office of Education. Hempstead, N. Y.: Hofstra University, 1965.

159. Sprague, N. F. "Inquiry Dialogue in the Classroom." Paper presented at Annual Conference of American Educational Research Association, New York, 1971.

160. Stallings, J. A., and Kaskowitz, D. H. "A Study of Follow Through Implementation." Paper presented at Annual Conference of American Educational Research Association, Washington, D.C., 1975.

161. Steele, J. M., et al. "An Instrument for Assessing Instructional Climate Through Low-Inference Student Judgments." *American Educational Research Journal* 8:447–66; 1971.

162. Stern, G. G., et al. *Methods in Personality Assessment.* Glencoe, Ill.: Free Press, 1956.

163. Stevens, R. *The Question as a Measure of Efficiency in Instruction: A Critical Study of Classroom Practices.* New York: Teachers College, Columbia University, Contributions to Education No. 48, 1912.

164. Stewart, L. G., and White, M. A. "Teacher Comments, Letter Grades, and Student Performance: What Do We Really Know?" *Journal of Educational Psychology* 68:488–500; 1977.

165. Thelen, J. N. "The Use of Advance Organizers and Guide Material in Viewing Science Motion Pictures in a Ninth Grade." Doctoral dissertation, Syracuse University, 1970.

166. Thomas, D. S. "An Attempt to Develop Precise Measurements in the Social Behavior Field." *Sociologus* 8:456; 1932.

167. Thompson, G. R., and Bowers, N. C. "Fourth Grade Achievement as Related to Creativity, Intelligence and Teaching Style." Paper presented at Annual Conference of American Educational Research Association, Chicago, 1968.

168. Tisher, R. P. "The Nature of Verbal Discourse in Classrooms and Association Between Verbal Discourse and Pupils' Understanding in Science." In *Scholars in Context: The Effect of Environments on Learning,* edited by W. J. Campbell, pp. 369–87. Sydney: Wiley, 1970.

169. Torrance, E. P. *Characteristics of Mathematics Teachers That Affect Students' Learning.* Project No. 1020, U.S. Office of Education. Minneapolis: University of Minnesota, 1966.

170. Traverse, R. M. W., ed. *Second Handbook of Research on Teaching.* Chicago: Rand McNally College Publishing Co., 1973.

171. Trickett, E. J., and Moos, R. H. *Assessment of the Psychosocial Environment of the High School Classroom.* Stanford, Calif.: Stanford University School of Medicine, 1971.

172. Walberg, H. J., ed. *Evaluating Educational Performance.* Berkeley, Calif.: McCutchan Publishing Corp., 1974.

173. ———. "Models for Optimizing and Individualizing School Learning." *Interchange* 3:15–27; 1971.

174. ———. "Predicting Class Learning: An Approach to the Class as a Social System." *American Educational Research Journal* 6:529–42; 1969.

175. ———, and Anderson, G. J. "Properties of the Achieving Urban Classes." *Journal of Educational Psychology* 63:381–85; 1972.

176. ———, and Thomas, S. C. "Open Education: An Operational Definition." *American Educational Research Journal* 9:197–208; 1972.

177. Wallen, N. E. *Relationships Between Teacher Characteristics and Student Behavior: Part 3.* Project No. 2628, U.S. Office of Education. Salt Lake City: University of Utah, 1966.

178. ———, and Wodtke, K. H. *Relationships Between Teacher Characteristics*

and Student Behavior: Part 1. Project No. 2-10-013, U.S. Office of Education. Salt Lake City: University of Utah, 1963.

179. Weber, W. A. "Relationships Between Teacher Behavior and Pupil Creativity in the Elementary School." Doctoral dissertation, Temple University, 1968.

180. Weiner, B., and Kukla, A. "An Attributional Analysis of Achievement Motivation." *Journal of Personality and Social Psychology* 15:1–20; 1970.

181. Welch, W. W., and Walberg, H. S. "Pre-Tests and Sensitization Effects in Curriculum Evaluation." *American Educational Research Journal* 7:605–14; 1970.

182. Westbury, I., and Bellack, A. A., eds. *Research into Classroom Processes.* New York: Teachers College Press, Teachers College, Columbia University, 1971.

183. Wirtz, W., et al. *On Further Examination.* New York: College Entrance Examination Board, 1977.

184. Withall, J. "The Development of a Technique for the Measurement of Social Emotional Climate in Classrooms." *Journal of Experimental Education* 17:347–61; 1949.

185. Wodarski, J. S., et al. "Individual Consequences Versus Different Shared Consequences Contingent on the Performance of Low-Achieving Group Members." *Journal of Applied Social Psychology* 3:276–90; 1973.

186. Wolfson, M. L. "A Consideration of Direct and Indirect Teaching Styles with Respect to Achievement and Retention of Learning in Science Classes." *Journal of Research in Science Teaching* 10:285–90; 1973.

187. Woolfolk, A. E. "Student Learning and Performance Under Varying Conditions of Teacher Verbal and Nonverbal Evaluative Communication." *Journal of Educational Psychology* 80:87–94; 1978.

188. Wright, C. J., and Nuthall, G. "Relationship Between Teacher Behavior and Pupil Achievement in Three Experimental Elementary Science Lessons." *American Educational Research Journal* 7:477–91; 1970.

189. Zahorik, J. A. "Classroom Feedback Behavior of Teachers." *Journal of Educational Research* 62:147–50; 1968.

190. ———. "Teacher Verbal Behavior: Perceived Value, Source of Acquisition, and Method of Justification." *Journal of Teacher Education* 28:50–55; 1977.

191. ———. "Teacher Verbal Feedback and Content Development." *Journal of Educational Research* 63:419–23; 1970.

ADDITIONAL RESOURCES FROM NEA

Brain Research and Learning
Computers in the Classroom, Henry S. Kepner, Jr., Editor
Interpersonal Communication by Paul G. Friedman
Lesson Planning for Meaningful Variety by Richard M. Henak
Motivation and Teaching by Raymond J. Wlodkowski
Nonverbal Communication by Patrick W. Miller
Questioning Skills, for Teachers by William W. Wilen
Student Team Learning by Robert E. Slavin
Teacher Self-Assessment by Gerald D. Bailey
The Teaching and Learning Process by Terry W. Blue